History of Britain
Alfred the Great

Brenda Williams

Illustrated by John James

HAMLYN

HISTORY OF BRITAIN – ALFRED THE GREAT
was produced for Hamlyn Children's Books
by Lionheart Books, London

Editor: Lionel Bender
Designer: Ben White
Editorial Assistants: Madeleine Samuel, Jo Hanks
Picture Researcher: Jennie Karrach
Media Conversion and Typesetting:
  Peter MacDonald

Educational Consultant: Jane Shuter
Editorial Advisors: Andrew Farrow, Paul Shuter

Production Controller: Catherine Bald
Editorial Director: David Riley

First published in Great Britain in 1995
by Hamlyn Children's Books,
an imprint of Reed International Books,
Michelin House, 81 Fulham Road, London SW3 6RB,
and Auckland, Melbourne, Singapore and Toronto.

Copyright © 1995 Reed International Books Limited

All rights reserved. No part of this publication may be reproduced, stored in a retrieval system or transmitted, in any form or by any means, electronic, mechanical, photocopying, recording or otherwise, without the prior permission of the copyright holders.

ISBN 0 600 587 800 Hb
ISBN 0 600 587 819 Pb

British Library Cataloguing-in-Publication Data.
A catalogue record for this book is available
from the British Library.

Printed in China

Acknowledgements
All illustrations by John James except maps, by Hayward Art Group.
Picture credits
AMO = Ashmolean Museum, Oxford. BAL = The Bridgeman Art Library. BLO = Bodleian Library, Oxford.
l = left, r = right, t = top, b = bottom, c = centre.
Pages: 4bl: The Board of Trinity College Dublin. 4tr: AMO. 5b, 6bl: By Courtesy of the Trustees of the British Museum, London. 6tr: British Library/Cotton Tib. B.V. pt1, f4v. 7t: BAL/Bibliotheque Nationale, Paris. 7cr: BLO/ Roll. 172E/28 Junius II p.56. 8bl: British Library/Cotton Claude B.IV-f24v. 8cr: Society of Antiquaries, London. 9br: Museum of London, PH94/346. 10bl: Michael Holford. 10br: AMO. 10tr: Winchester Museums Service. 11tr: Courtesy of the Trustees of the Victoria and Albert Museum, London 12l: British Library/Cotton Tib. C.VI- f9. 13t: University Museum of National Antiquities, Oslo, Norway. 13b: British Library/ Cotton Tib.B.V. pt. 1 – f5v. 14bl: AMO. 15t: Courtesy of the Master and Fellows of Corpus Christi College, Cambridge. 16tl: Michael Holford. 16br: University of Bergen, Norway. 17tl: BLO/MS. Junius.11, page 66. 18tr: Hunting Aerofilms Limited. 19c: British Library/Cotton Claud BIV, f59. MC. 19tr: British Library/Cotton Claud. DII-f8. 20bl: AMO. 20-21: BLO/Ms. Hatton 20. fol.1v. 21tl: The Pierpont Morgan Libary/Art Resource, NY/M.736, f.9v. 21tr: British Library/Add 34,890-f.10v. 22cl: Royal Library, Stockholm, Sweden/Cod. Holm A.135, fol.11r. 22tr, cr, br: AMO. Cover: Artwork by John James. Icons by Michael Shoebridge. Photos: British Library/Cotton Tib. B.V. pt1, f4v (Battling Saxons), British Library/Cotton Claud B.IV-f24v (The Witan), AMO (jewel).

PLACES TO VISIT

Here are some museums and sites connected with Alfred the Great you can visit.

Ashmolean Museum, Oxford. Displays the Alfred jewel, Saxon sword hilt.
Bodleian Library, Oxford. Has a manuscript of Alfred's Pastoral Rule.
British Library, London. Illuminated (decorated) manuscript books of Saxon times are kept here.
British Museum, London. Ethelwulf's ring and other finds.
Cheddar, Somerset. The site of a Saxon king's hall.
Museum of London, London. Has Viking weapons and other finds.
Sompting, West Sussex. Saxon church tower.
Uffington, Oxfordshire. The White Horse on the downs here is traditionally associated with the Ashdown battle, but is older.
Wallingford, Oxfordshire. Example of a Saxon town.
Wantage, Berkshire. Alfred's birthplace, with a statue of Alfred (1877).
Wareham, Dorset. Another Saxon town.
Winchester, Hampshire. Alfred's capital, has a statue of him, also a museum and cathedral.
York, Yorkshire. Visit the Jorvik Museum of Viking life.

Information about Alfred's life and reign comes mainly from the *Life of Alfred*, written by the monk Asser, who was the king's friend and advisor and who died about 909. Another source is the *Anglo-Saxon Chronicle*, a history of the English people which was begun in Alfred's reign and which may have been suggested by him. It is not completely reliable when dealing with early dates.

INTRODUCTION

Alfred is one of the most admired kings in British history. He grew up in the AD 850s as his kingdom of Wessex was in danger of being overrun by the Vikings. By fighting his enemies, he saved his land. By making peace with them, he ensured the survival of his kingdom and the culture of Anglo-Saxon England. After Alfred, the kings of Wessex became the kings of England, the nation he had helped found. Alfred let Vikings settle peaceably on English land. This example was followed over many centuries, as Britain took in peoples from other nations and cultures. Kings after Alfred ruled bigger kingdoms, and even empires, but none of them earned his title – the Great.

CONTENTS

ALFRED'S ENGLAND 4 *Silver cup from Cornwall, about AD 875*	DEFENDING THE REALM 16 *Top of Saxon sword handle, about 900*
ALFRED'S BOYHOOD 6 *9th-century statue of Charlemagne*	LAWMAKER AND GUARDIAN 18 *Coin struck in 886 to show recapture of London*
THE YOUNG SOLDIER 8 *Danish silver penny made in London*	SCHOLAR AND TEACHER 20 *Bradford on Avon church*
ALFRED THE KING 10 *Bronze seal die of Bishop of Suffolk, about 850*	AFTER ALFRED 22 *Jewelled top of pointer*
HIDING FROM THE DANES 12 *King Alfred coin, about 875*	GLOSSARY – DEFINITIONS OF IMPORTANT WORDS 23
ALFRED THE PEACEMAKER 14 *Drinking horn, about 890*	TIMECHART 23
	INDEX 24

ALFRED'S ENGLAND

Alfred was born in 849 into the royal family that ruled the kingdom of the West Saxons – Wessex – in southern England. His ancestors had ruled their English lands for 300 years, after seizing them from the Britons of the southwest. Wessex was one of several English kingdoms set up by Angles and Saxons who had invaded from Europe.

Wessex had become a strong kingdom. In 815, its king, Egbert, defeated the Britons of Devon and Cornwall. Then he took control of Kent, Sussex and Essex. He gained the important kingdom of Mercia in 829 and soon Northumbria, too, accepted him as leader. Mercia had won back its freedom by the time Egbert died in 839. But for a while, the king of Wessex had been bretwalda, or overlord, of all the English. Alfred was this soldier-king's grandson.

▷ **A coin of Ethelwulf, Alfred's father.**
Ethelwulf celebrated Alfred's birth, as shown here. Ethelwulf kept his kingdom together, despite family quarrels. Such feuds had led to civil war in other English kingdoms. In 856, Ethelwulf's son Ethelbald took his father's throne. But Ethelwulf ruled eastern Wessex until his death in 858.

▷ **The *Book of Kells*** was made around 800 by monks in Ireland or Northumbria.
● The Church and its learning linked the Christian peoples of Europe.
● Before becoming king of Wessex, Egbert lived for a time in exile with Charlemagne, king of the Franks. The Northumbrian monk Alcuin came to Charlemagne's court and brought the learning of scholars from his homeland to France.

4

◁ **Map of Europe in the mid-800s** showing the kingdoms of England.
● Across the North Sea in Scandinavia were the Viking lands of Norway, Sweden and Denmark.
● The first Viking ships brought raiders to Wessex in 787.
● Vikings plundered the rich monasteries of Northumbria and raided round the English coast.
● In 838, Cornish Britons joined Vikings to attack Wessex. Egbert defeated them, but the Vikings came back.

Alfred was born at Wantage, in what is now Oxfordshire. The atheling, or prince, was the youngest of King Ethelwulf's five sons.

The English kings were still fighting among themselves, but they also faced a common enemy. Fierce Viking warriors from Scandinavia were attacking from the sea and setting up bases from which to make further raids inland. Ethelwulf spent most of his reign fighting to keep the Vikings – or Danes, as the English called them – out of Wessex. He won a big victory in 851 against a Viking army that had raided London and Canterbury and had put the king of Mercia to flight. But the Vikings always came back. Alfred's brothers were also fighting off their attacks. Athelstan, the oldest, was given eastern Wessex (parts of present-day Kent, Surrey, Sussex and Essex) to rule.

△ **Gold rings** (top) of King Ethelwulf and (right) of his daughter Ethelswith.

ALFRED'S BOYHOOD

Saxon kings moved about their kingdoms with their household servants and guards. Young Alfred lived with the court, learning how to ride, to fight and be a good lord. When he was four, he had his first great adventure. He went to Rome in Italy.

▽ **Feasting in a royal hall.** The king's court was a centre for feasting, music, story-telling and greeting guests from other kingdoms.

The Saxons of England were Christians of the Catholic Church, led by the Pope in Rome. The Church's bishops, priests and monks were the most learned people in the land, and most English kings tried to keep on good terms with the Pope. In 853, Ethelwulf sent Alfred to Italy, to see Pope Leo IV. Leo treated his young visitor with respect. He was godfather to Alfred at his confirmation ceremony, and gave the young prince the title and robes of a Roman consul. (Consuls were involved in government, law and order in the Roman Empire.)

Alfred was a bright boy, liked by all. At home in Wessex, he loved to be outdoors, hunting and hawking. He also enjoyed supper afterwards in his father's royal hall.

It was in the great hall that he heard minstrels sing songs about the old Saxon heroes and the battles they fought. Soon he knew the poems by heart. Alfred won from his mother, Osburh, an illuminated manuscript, a beautifully decorated book which she said she would give to the first of her sons able to read it to her. Alfred asked his tutor to read the book, learned every word and recited it back to his mother. In 855, Alfred returned to Rome for a year, this time with his father Ethelwulf. Athelstan had died in 850 so Ethelbald ruled Wessex while they were away.

Reverse side / Front side

◁ **Silver sixpences** made in Alfred's reign as part of the king's yearly payments to the Pope. Ethelwulf ordered his successors to send these gifts.

◁ **Charles the Bald, King of the West Franks.** Ethelwulf and Alfred stayed with Charles on their way home from Rome in 856. By this time, Alfred's mother, Osburh, must have been dead, for Ethelwulf married Charles's 12-year-old daughter, Judith.

When they came back to Britain, Ethelbald refused to give back the throne to his father but let him rule eastern Wessex.

△ **This Saxon drawing** shows a noble family at home in their hall. Alfred probably lived in a hall like this.

◁ **Alfred meets Pope Leo at the Vatican.** The Pope gave Alfred a sword as a symbol of the ancient link between Rome and England.

THE YOUNG SOLDIER

Alfred came home to find his older brothers facing the biggest Viking attacks yet made against England. Each brother fought to keep the crown of Wessex as their kingdom was raided, but not conquered. The rest of the English kingdoms fell to the Great Army of Vikings that landed in 865.

After Ethelbald died in 860, his brother Ethelbert became king of Wessex. During this reign, Viking raiders plundered the Wessex capital of Winchester. But the ealdormen (local leaders) of Berkshire and Hampshire called out their men to fight, cut off the Vikings from their ships and defeated them.

When Ethelbert died in 866 his brother Ethelred became king. Now the English faced the full fury of the Vikings. The Great Army was led by Ivar Boneless and Halfdan. They landed in East Anglia, where they forced King Edmund to make peace on their terms. Then they rounded up horses, rode to Northumbria, killed its rulers and set up a base at York.

In 868 the Great Army invaded Mercia and seized Nottingham. The king of Mercia, who was married to Ethelred's sister, now called on his brother-in-law for help.

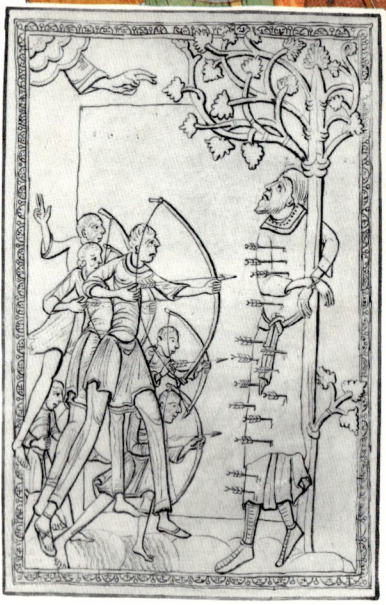

△ **The death of King Edmund of East Anglia in 869.** He is shown being shot with arrows, and probably suffered even worse tortures. By 895 Edmund was honoured as a saint in East Anglia. November 20 was remembered as the day of his death.

◁ **A Saxon king (top left) and his warriors** battle against Vikings.

Ethelred took an army north, and with him went 19-year-old Alfred. Although they did well, their ally, the king of Mercia, made peace with the Vikings. In 869 the Great Army overran East Anglia and killed King Edmund. Then it turned on Wessex.

By the spring of 871, Ethelred and Alfred had fought five battles. In a raid on the Danish base at Reading, they were beaten off and driven across Berkshire by the Great Army. But when they reached the great chalk ridge called Ashdown, the English turned to face their enemies.

They won a famous victory, slaying one of the Danish kings and sending the Great Army fleeing back to Reading. But two weeks later, Ethelred and Alfred were again defeated. In April 871, Ethelred died. He left a baby son, but Wessex needed a soldier to lead it. Alfred became king.

△ **The Battle of Ashdown** was fought below the ancient White Horse of Uffington, cut into the chalk hillside. The Danes held the higher ground, with their army in two groups. The English also split their army. Ethelred faced one group of Danes and Alfred led his men against the other group.

Ethelred was still at morning prayers when Alfred attacked the Danes. With the battle raging, Ethelred led his men to victory.

△ **Sea routes of Viking invaders to southern England.** The weapons below are two Viking battle-axe heads and an iron spearhead.

ALFRED THE KING

"And during that year (871) nine general engagements were fought against the Danish army in the kingdom south of the Thames... And that year nine (Danish) earls were killed and one king. And the West Saxons made peace with the enemy..."

The story of the battle for Wessex is told in the *Anglo-Saxon Chronicle*, a yearly history begun in King Alfred's reign. Viking raiders struck at once, while Alfred was at his brother's funeral. Then the young king lost a battle at Wilton, and had to ask for peace. The invaders agreed. They had struggled to win battles in Wessex, and left to find weaker prey.

Alfred was crowned king when it seemed he might well lose his kingdom. He had a wife, Elswitha, and a young son. To pass on his crown, Alfred had to organize his battle-weary warriors for the next Viking attack – whenever it might come.

△ **A Saxon bone carving** called the Winchester Angels. Alfred's Winchester was a centre for learning. Work on the city's New Minster (church) began in Alfred's reign. The king founded Hyde Abbey, north of the city, where he was married. (Here, Alfred rides to the Abbey). His wife Elswitha founded the convent of Nunnaminster.

◁ **A typical Saxon church**, at Earls Barton, Northamptonshire.

▽ **A silver penny** made in Winchester during Alfred's reign.

10

▷ **Bone or ivory comb** from a Saxon bishop's regalia. Alfred's crowning as king was a Church ceremony.

In 875, the Great Army of Vikings divided. One group moved north to Northumbria. The rest followed their leader, Guthrum, to East Anglia. Then, in 876, Guthrum decided to attack Wessex.

The armies of Alfred and Guthrum fought, agreed a truce, and fought again. Alfred's army was the smaller, and the peasant soldiers called up to join the Wessex fyrd (militia) were not full-time fighters like the Vikings. Sooner or later they went home to their farms. At the end of the summer in 877, Guthrum agreed to leave Wessex. The fyrd soldiers went home for the winter. After Christmas, the Danes struck.

Hiding from the Danes

"...the (Viking) host went secretly in midwinter after Twelfth Night to Chippenham and rode over Wessex and occupied it...", says the chronicler. Many Wessex people were driven overseas, he says. The rest surrendered to the Danes, "except Alfred the king".

▽ **A Saxon noble soldier**, with shield and spear. Other weapons were axes, bows and swords. Alfred's men wore little armour and fought on foot, shoulder to shoulder, forming a "shield wall" against the enemy.

▽ **Building the fort on Athelney.** Alfred's men drive tree trunks into the boggy ground to make a stockade. Houses are inside the walls. The king supervises the work, adding his knowledge of forts seen while fighting outside Wessex. One story from his time on Athelney tells how Alfred went into Guthrum's camp disguised as a minstrel, to gain information.

Saxon kingdoms found it hard to resist Viking raids. They had smaller armies and poorer communications. But Alfred's loyal soldiers fought well from their defended base.

▷ **Overland, a Viking army** used captured horses and supply carts – as in this picture made from tapestry pieces found in a Viking ship burial in Norway.

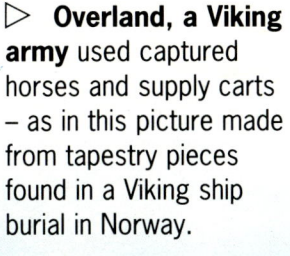

△ **Illustration from a Saxon calendar.** At harvest-time, soldiers from the fyrd went back to their farms. They also stopped fighting for the winter. Unfortunately the Vikings did not.

It seemed that Guthrum had won Wessex. But Alfred "with a small force, moved under difficulties through woods and into...places in the marshes". With a few loyal followers, Alfred hid on an island called Athelney in the Somerset marshes. There they built a fort. Alfred had seen how the Danes set up bases from which to raid their enemies. He would do the same. Others in the west kept fighting, too. A Viking fleet of 23 ships was lost to men from Devon, who captured its prized "raven" banner, said to flutter before a Viking victory and droop before defeat. While Alfred was free, Wessex fought back.

From Alfred's hiding in Athelney come famous stories, which may be partly true. The best-known story tells how the king – preparing bows and arrows in the shelter of a cowherd's hut – is scolded by the peasant's wife for letting her bread burn.

Alfred and his men spent the spring of 878 at Athelney, making several hit-and-run raids. Then in May, the king "rode to Ecgbrytesstan (Egbert's stone), and came to meet him there all the men of Somerset and Wiltshire and...part of Hampshire...and they greeted him warmly". Two days later he marched to Edington, where "...he fought against the entire host, and put it to flight."

13

Alfred the Peacemaker

Alfred's victory at Edington, north of Salisbury Plain in Wiltshire, was his most vital. In a peace bargain with Guthrum he gained two important agreements. The Viking leader promised to leave Wessex – and this time kept his word. He also agreed to become a Christian, like the English.

▷ **Alfred welcomes Guthrum** into his hall at the Viking leader's christening ceremony.
● Alfred took hostages to make sure the Vikings kept the peace.
● Alfred showed mercy and statesmanship in acting as godfather to Guthrum, who now owed him the duty of an adopted son.
● Guthrum ruled in East Anglia until his death in 890.

▽ **A coin of Guthrum**, minted when Guthrum became king of East Anglia. It carries his new Christian name (Edelia or Athelstan).

△ **A copy of the peace treaty** made between Alfred and Guthrum. This agreement did not end the fighting for good, but shows how important Alfred had become.
● Alfred is called the leader and spokesman of "all councillors of the English race".
● By the late 880s, Alfred is named in charters (legal papers) as "King of the English". One of his coins bore this title for the first time on an English coin.
● Asser, who wrote Alfred's life-story, called him "Ruler of all Christians in the island of Britain, king of the Angles and Saxons". Alfred himself first used the name "Angelcynn", "English people".

Alfred's army chased the enemy from Edington back to their camp at Chippenham. There the English besieged Guthrum's fort for two weeks, until the Vikings gave in. A week later, Guthrum and 30 of his men were baptised Christians at Aller on the River Parret. Alfred acted as Guthrum's godfather.

The Viking leader then spent 12 days at Wedmore in Somerset in peace talks with his Wessex host. The result was an agreement, called the Treaty of Wedmore, which gave the Vikings the part of England that lay north and east of a line running roughly from London to Chester. Lands south and east remained with Wessex. By autumn 880, the Danes had left Wessex to begin settling in East Anglia, with Guthrum as their king. It was the end of the Great Army in Wessex, but not the end of the Vikings in England.

Even as Guthrum's army moved north-east, a new Viking force gathered offshore. Its ships rowed up the River Thames and its men spent the winter of 878 at Fulham. The next winter they crossed the Channel to attack the West Franks. Some then returned to Kent in 884 and besieged Rochester, until Alfred came to the rescue. The Vikings left, only to make more raids south of the Thames.

'Peaceful' Vikings from East Anglia had given help to the new invaders, so Alfred sent a fleet to raid their settlements. In 886 the king captured London from the Danes, "after the burning of towns and the slaughter of peoples". Now, "all the English people submitted to Alfred except those...under the power of the Danes."

DEFENDING THE REALM

By capturing London, Alfred had shown that land held by the Vikings could be won back. To keep such lands, he had to make Wessex secure. He needed a strong army, navy and land defences. He started by building new and bigger ships.

◁ **Viking treasure** found in a chest at Cuerdale near the River Ribble in Lancashire in 1840. Many of the 7,000 silver coins were from Alfred's reign. The Cuerdale Treasure is the largest Viking hoard ever found in northwest Europe.

To attack the Vikings at sea was Alfred's first line of defence. According to the Chronicle, he ordered ships of a new design "neither on the Frisian nor the Danish pattern". We do not know what Alfred's ships were like, except that they were bigger than Viking ships, and had 60 oars. Alfred had experience of sea fights – in 875 he had led a fleet against seven Danish ships, capturing one.

To fight the Vikings more successfully on land and stop the kingdom being taken by surprise – as so often before – Alfred reorganized his army. He divided the fyrd into two groups. While half the men were serving as soldiers, the rest were free to look after their farms, and guard forts. If the Vikings attacked, the men under arms were ready to fight, led by the nobles, who were full-time soldiers. Soldiers in reserve would then join the army, if needed.

△ **A bronze book cover** made in Northumbria in the 8th century and stolen by Vikings. It was found in a Viking grave in Norway.

To defend his realm, Alfred ordered the building of forts and fortified towns, known as burhs (from which we get the word 'boroughs'). Anyone who held land had to help build and look after these defences. No village was more than a day's march from a burh. Some were based on old Roman fortifications. Others were new defences of earth banks and walls.

In 892, 300 Viking ships landed two armies in England. Alfred's son Edward now fought beside his father. The fyrd soldiers gathered swiftly, and this time pursued the enemy, rather than turning for home. In 895 Vikings raided farms along the Thames and Lea rivers. Alfred blocked the rivers to stop their ships escaping, and built two forts. The raiders were driven off.

△ **Manuscript drawing of Noah's Ark** showing the outline of new English ships.

▽ **Alfred's new navy** leaves harbour. The new ships were like Viking longships but were faster, steadier and had higher sides.

Lawmaker and Guardian

During Alfred's reign, Wessex was never free from the Viking threat. But the king's new forts, and his changes to the army and navy, gave the kingdom more confidence. Alfred then tried to improve his people's lives in other ways. He made new laws and set up plans for his people's education.

▷ **Map of the lands in England settled by Danes**, which later became known as the Danelaw. Many place names in this area, such as those ending in -by, (town) – like Grimsby – or -thorpe (small village), are Scandinavian, showing where the Danes made their homes.

▷ **Wareham, in Dorset**, was one of Alfred's new burhs. It was protected by an earth bank still visible today (top of photo).

Alfred based his new laws on what he thought were the best from earlier law codes. He wrote: "For I dared not presume to set in writing at all many of my own... But those which I found anywhere which seemed to me most just ...I collected... Then I, Alfred, showed these to all my councillors, and they then said that they were pleased to observe them".

Alfred's law code was the first issued by an English king for 100 years and the first drawn up for English people from Wessex to the Northumbrian border. The most important laws dealt with the right of sanctuary, the blood feud, and penalties for breaking an oath. They stress how a man must be loyal to his lord, but also give some protection for the weak against the strong. "Judge thou very fairly. Do not judge one judgement for the rich and another for the poor; nor one for the one more dear and another for the one more hateful".

△ **Alfred and Guthrum agreed a new treaty in 886.** This copy shows Alfred on his throne. The treaty agreed that Danes and English were to be treated equally by law.

◁ **Saxon kings and their witan**, a council of nobles and churchmen, made laws and decided punishments. The witan also elected the king.

◁ **Four men were needed to defend** every 5 metres of wall or earthwork in a burh. Each district had to supply its local fort with one man for every hide (an area of land) it covered. When an attack came, people rounded up their livestock and made for the safety of the nearest burh.

After Alfred captured London in 886, most English people saw him as their leader. Scholars and churchmen came to his court. They gave him advice in making "the peace which King Alfred and King Guthrum and the councillors of all the English race and all the people which is in East Anglia have all agreed on".

London had belonged to the kingdom of Mercia before being captured by the Danes. Alfred gave it back to Ethelred, the ealdorman of Mercia, who had bravely led his men against their enemies. By so doing, Alfred gained a strong and loyal ally. Alfred's daughter Ethelflaeda became Ethelred's wife, which strengthened this allegiance.

Scholar and Teacher

Alfred said a king needed "men who pray, and soldiers and workmen". He had created well-trained soldiers and sailors and started his system of forts. Now he wanted to educate his churchmen and people. Alfred himself was almost 40 when he learnt to read Latin, the language of scholars and the Church.

Visitors came to Alfred's court from far and wide. Letters came from as far as Jerusalem. The king also sent for learned men to help make his court a centre for art and education, like Charlemagne's before him. Among Alfred's scholars were Plegmund, who became Archbishop of Canterbury, Grimbald from Rheims (France) and Asser from Wales. Asser became Alfred's friend and wrote about his life.

▷ **Opening page of Alfred's translation of the *Pastoral Rule*.** The first line says "this book shall (go) to Wiogora Ceastre (Worcester)". It goes on: "King Alfred sends greeting to Bishop Waerferth in loving words...".

▷ **The Alfred Jewel**, found near Athelney in 1693, bears the words 'Alfred had me made'. It may be part of an aestel, a pointer or bookmark, that Alfred said he was sending with each copy of the *Pastoral Rule* to every cathedral in his kingdom. Books (manuscripts) in Alfred's day had to be copied out by hand. Such painstaking work, done by monks in monasteries, was disrupted by Viking raids. Alfred encouraged the production of clearly written manuscripts, and many fine books were made at Winchester.

◁ **Alfred's kingdom** was under constant threat from Viking attacks from the sea, as this Saxon picture of Viking longships of the time shows clearly.

▷ **A decorated page from the Grimbald Gospels**, made in Canterbury or Winchester long after Alfred's death. Grimbald was a scholar from France who acted as a foreign advisor to Alfred.

Alfred wanted English priests to understand both Latin and English, and young English people to learn to read their own language. Then he planned to translate into English those books "most necessary for all men to know". The king had a high regard for learning and wisdom. He ordered his judges to learn to read, or give up their work.

Alfred did translate his books. Among them was the *Pastoral Rule*, written by Pope Gregory the Great. Alfred sent a copy to every cathedral in his kingdom and for centuries this book was looked on as a guide for priests. Alfred also tried to set up monasteries again in England, for their learning and libraries had been lost to Viking raids.

In his last years Alfred was concerned with how a good ruler should govern his people. The king died on 26 October 899. He had fought for 30 years to save his kingdom, out of which grew the English nation. He is the only king the English call 'the Great'.

◁ **Alfred checks a page of a manuscript** produced by monks in Winchester Cathedral. Pages, made of parchment, were bound in leather covers.

21

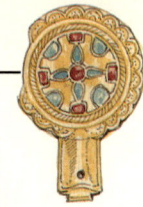

AFTER ALFRED

Alfred left the witan to decide who should be king after his death. This council of important nobles and church leaders had to choose between Ethelwold, Alfred's nephew, and Edward, Alfred's son. Edward had already proved a brave and successful soldier. He was elected king of Wessex.

Edward (899-924)

Athelstan (924-940)

▷ **Coins of Edward and his sons**, Athelstan and Edmund. These three kings regained lands lost to the Danes.
● Alfred's grandson Athelstan fought as far north as Scotland. He ruled both English and Danes in England, and was famous in Europe.
● The reign of Edward's grandson, Edgar (959-975) brought peace and the "golden age" of Anglo-Saxon England.

◁ **The *Codex Aureus*** is a Gospel Book, made in Kent before Alfred was born. Seized by Vikings, it was bought back by an English noble.

Edmund (940-946)

Ethelwold rebelled and fled to join the Vikings of Northumbria. In 902 he gathered an army of Danes from East Anglia to attack Mercia and Wessex. Edward then marched into Danish land. Both sides had now crossed the frontier agreed between Alfred and Guthrum.

Alfred had defended his kingdom. Edward now attacked, to win land back from the Danes, aided by Ethelred of Mercia and his wife Ethelflaeda.

Ethelflaeda, "Lady of the Mercians", joined her brother Edward in leading raids and building burhs. Some land was won in battle, some bought from the Danes with gold. By the end of Edward's reign, he controlled all Danes south of the Humber. Welsh princes, the kings of the Scots and the leaders of the Northumbrians also obeyed him. Edward "the Elder", son of Alfred of Wessex, was overlord of all England.

Glossary

abbey church or community headed by an abbot.
atheling Saxon prince.
banner flag, carried in battle.
baptism making someone a member of the Christian Church.
blood-feud quarrel between families.
Britons people who were living in Britain before the Saxon invasions.
burh fortified town.
Celts people who settled in Britain from 500 BC.
code (of laws) set of laws made by a ruler.
confirmation Christian ceremony of declaring faith, usually for young people.

Danes English name for Vikings from Denmark or often for all Vikings.
ealdorman high-ranking nobleman, the leader of an English district.
Franks people living in what are now France and Germany.
fyrd English army, of part-time soldiers.
godfather man acting like a father to newly baptised Christian.
hostage person held captive, either for ransom or as part of a peace agreement.
Latin language of the ancient Romans, used by scholars in Europe throughout the Middle Ages.

lord noble or king, a person who was owed loyalty by his followers.
manuscript book copied by hand, usually by monks, and often illuminated or decorated.
minster large church or cathedral.
monastery buildings in which monks live and work.
sanctuary place of refuge, such as a church, where a person was safe from capture.
tapestry picture made from woven threads.
Vatican headquarters of the Pope in Rome.
White horses figures cut in chalk downs of England.

▷ **Map showing the major towns** mentioned in this book.

Timechart

787 Vikings land in Wessex for the first time.

793 Vikings terrorize Northumbria, looting Lindisfarne monastery.

849 Alfred born at Wantage.

851 Vikings plunder London and Canterbury.

853 Alfred goes to Rome.

855 Alfred's second trip to Rome, with his father King Ethelwulf.

865 Great Army of Vikings invades eastern, central and northern England. Alfred fights alongside his brother, King Ethelred.

869 Vikings kill King Edmund of East Anglia.

871 Battle of Ashdown won by Ethelred and Alfred. Soon after, Alfred becomes king of Wessex.

872 Vikings make London their base.

875 Alfred wins a small sea victory.

876 Guthrum leads large Viking attack on Wessex.

878 Viking winter attack almost defeats Wessex. Alfred takes refuge on Athelney. Wins battle of Edington. Guthrum makes peace. Treaty of Wedmore.

886 Alfred captures London and makes it a burh.

892 Alfred spends his last seven years translating Latin books into English.

899 Alfred dies, on 26 October. His son Edward becomes king.

23

INDEX

Alcuin 4
Aller 15
Angles 4
Anglo-Saxon Chronicle, the 2, 10
army 11, 13, 16 *see also* Great Army, soldiers
Ashdown, Battle of 9, 23
Asser 15, 20
Athelney 12, 13, 20, 23
Athelstan 5, 14, 22

battles 5, 8, 9, 10, 11, 14, 15, 16, 23
Berkshire 8, 9
books (manuscripts) 4, 13, 20, 21, 23
bretwalda 4
Britons 4, 5, 23
burhs 17, 18, 19, 23

Canterbury 5, 21
Charlemagne 3, 4, 20
Charles the Bald 7
Chippenham 12, 15
Christians and the Church 3, 4, 6, 10, 11, 14, 16, 19, 20, 21
Codex Aureus 22
coins 3, 4, 6, 10, 14, 15, 16, 22
Cornwall 4
court life 6, 20
Cuerdale Treasure 16

Danelaw, the 18
Danes, the 5, 9, 10, 18, 19, 22
Denmark 5
Devon 4

ealdormen 8
East Anglia 8, 9, 11, 14, 15, 19, 22, 23
Edelia 14

Edgar 22
Edington 13, 14, 15, 23
Edmund 8, 9, 22, 23
education and learning 6, 18, 20, 21
Edward 17, 22, 23
Egbert 4, 5
Elswitha 10
England and the English 5, 8, 9, 14, 15, 18, 19, 22
Essex 4, 7
Ethelbald 4, 6, 7, 8
Ethelbert 8
Ethelflaeda 19, 22
Ethelred 2, 9, 19, 22, 23
Ethelswith 5
Ethelwold 22
Ethelwulf 4, 5, 6, 7, 20, 23

feasting 6
forts 12, 13, 17 *see also* fyrds, burhs
Franks, the 4, 7
fyrds 11, 13, 16, 17, 23

Great Army, the 8, 9, 11, 15
Gregory the Great, Pope 21
Grimbald 20, 21
Guthrum 11, 12, 13, 14, 15, 19, 22

Halfdan 8
Hampshire 8
Hyde Abbey 10

Ivar Boneless 8

Jewel, the Alfred 20
Judith 7

Kent 4, 7, 15
King of the English 15

languages 20, 21, 23
laws 18, 19
Leo IV, Pope 6, 7
London 5, 15, 16, 19, 23

Mercia 4, 5, 8, 9, 19, 22
monasteries and monks 4, 5, 6, 21, 23
music 6

navy 17, 18
Northumbria 4, 5, 8, 11, 22, 23
Norway 5
Nottingham 8
Nunnaminster 10

Osburh 6, 7
Oxfordshire 2, 5

Pastoral Rule, the 20, 21
peace treaty 15, 19, 23
Plegmund 20

Reading 9

Saxons, the 3, 4, 7, 10, 11
Scotland 5, 22
ships 5, 13, 16, 17, 21
soldiers 11, 12, 13, 16, 17
Surrey 7
Sussex 2, 4, 7
Sweden 5

Vikings 3, 4, 5, 8, 10, 11, 12, 13, 14, 15, 16, 17, 18, 22

Wales 5
Wantage 2, 5, 23
Wareham 2, 18
weapons 9, 12, 16

Wedmore 15, 23
Wessex 3, 4, 5, 6, 7, 8, 9, 10, 11, 14, 18, 22
Witton 10
Winchester 2, 8, 10, 20, 21
witan, the 19, 22
Worcester 20

York 2, 8